Thoughts
✧ of the ✧
Mind

REGGIE NAPHTALI

Copyright © 2016 Reggie Naphtali
All rights reserved
First Edition

PAGE PUBLISHING, INC.
New York, NY

First originally published by Page Publishing, Inc. 2016

ISBN 978-1-68348-481-3 (pbk)
ISBN 978-1-68348-482-0 (digital)

Printed in the United States of America

Part I

POEMS
Portraits of Extreme Meditation Scribed

THOUGHTS OF THE MIND

AIDS

Another Indefinite Death Sentence

Extreme sufferation
Having no respect for anyone
A very costly, deadly infection
Lots of pain and severe physical tribulations
On top of the withdrawal and too often rejection
A lonesome life on medication
This disease touches the life of each and every one
In some cases, it's wiping out generations
Each human must take action
Don't look at the outward appearance
Safety must always be the only direction
Life's enduring regulations
Always in the warning, sexual precaution
The only true satisfaction
Love the protection
The real-life sensation

Destroying populations
Caution, be protective in all situations
It's your life-or-death decision
You've got your life in your hands
You're the one
Abstinence! If not, safe sex solution
Prepare, let it always be your intention
Safe sex, live long, passion

Live on
One partner, only one
Healthy and strong dedication
Self and partner protection
Don't be caught in the negative action
It must always be safe sex session
It's your only positive position
Construct positive reaction
At all times use protection
It's a lifetime weapon
Help to end the vast destruction
Don't put yourself in that grave isolation
Don't blame it on drugs and alcohol
AIDS
Another indefinite death sentence
It's a threat to the global population
Needed is your safe sex obligation
Protect yourself and your nation
Yield not to temptations

AS I GO THROUGH THIS LIFE

As I go through this life
I real eyes, He died and arise
To save our lives
Judah He identified, King David's royal tribe
Incarnated from on high
His name is Jesus Christ
The most powerful I, glorify
Never ever deny

As I go through this life
I've seen signs of the times
Like Marcus Garvey prophesied
A Davidic, Solomonic king was crowned
In these times
His Imperial Majesty Emperor Haile
Selassie I
Living an exemplary life
He opened our eyes
He continually exalted Jesus Christ
Declaring worldwide the Holy Bible
Is the rallying point for all mankind?
And a prophet did arise
King David's red eyes
Oh, ye Gadite, organize and centralize
Jacob's hive in the name of Jesus Christ
Keep the body alive

As I go through this life
Ye stiff-necked lost children, come alive
Repentance time
It's family-reunion time of the Israelites
Declaring minds only Jesus Christ can give
Life to the fullest heights
Spiritual light; born-again child
Accept ye the birthright
Children identify and live that life
Nations, it's time to glorify
Real eye sight; as you go through this life Jesus Christ
The way, the truth, the eternal light

BOYS

Brothers **of Y**our **S**ociety

Boys, young men to this world be a blessing
Stand up and responsibly play your part
Within the system
Don't live a life that you will end up in prison
Although you may face adverse situations
You must truly overcome and positively excel

Unto your parents, teachers, and elders
Show uttermost respect and honestly listen
In this life, you're to be the stronger vessel
Learn, adapt to all the inspiring lessons
Be an enlightened, educated role model
Don't act as if you're an agent of the devil
Please stay out of trouble
Live your life clean and humble
It's plain and simple
Work hard always, honestly reaching for the highest level

EDUCATION

Every **D**ay **u**nder **C**ommitted **A**ctions
Toward **I**mproving **O**ur **N**ation

Mankind stand at attention
And all ye nations with love
True love and uttermost of devotion
Regardless of race or religion
Let's all come forward, march on
To rid this world of poverty, segregation, wars, illiteracy
The different forms of abuses and oppression

Hoping these words touch the hearts of each and every one
Especially this younger generation
Stop now; love, look, listen, learn, and understand
We've got to bridge the gap between the youths
And the older generation
Surely between the rich and the poor man
Let's take all the appropriate actions
To better all the communications
And all the living conditions
Let's bring about peace to the global land
Out of many we hath to be just this one

THOUGHTS OF THE MIND

The road of life, it's so, so long
And filled with many, many tribulations
But, young man, young woman, please stand strong
Thou hath the backbone of nations
The future generation, you've got the Lord's words
And this world at your hands

Young man, young woman, know there is a spiritual and a material direction
So first give all thanks and all praises unto
Our Lord and Savior Jesus Christ, the Almighty One
The solid foundation
And be ye filled with spiritual inspiration
Seek ye positive vibrations
Always have that self-determination
Focus on your ambition
Set yourself concrete plans
Take all the opportunities at hand
And please get yourself a very, very good, good EDUCATION

EDUCATION
Every **d**ay **u**nder **c**ommitted **a**ctions
Toward **i**mproving **o**ur **n**ation
It's so essential
Its collective survival
In a world of competition
And computerized nations
With great, great scientific inventions
Young man, young woman, you need a very, very good, good EDUCATION

Young man, young woman, stop the self-destruction
Down, down with all the drugs and all the notorious gangs
Its precious life you a gang bang
You can't fight life with drugs and weapons in your hands
Why choose to be a living-dead human
The drugs and the weapons are mostly for
the destruction of the poor man
Don't be part of the evil plan
Come let us strive to make this world a better homeland
It's mankind's only reservation
Don't come add to all the pollution
Just come on and get yourself a very, very
good, good EDUCATION

Calling, begging, pleading, and praying that each and every man
Run, come join hearts in hands
For the unification of all these nations
Mankind, it's your obligation to rid your homeland
of hatred, poverty, racism, wars, and starvation
Equal rights and justice must rule throughout mankind's dominion
Oh, ye children of the Lord, come take con-
trol of this sad, sad situation
And help to preserve His holy creation
And as ye go along, just get yourself a very,
very good, good EDUCATION

And to all ye older ones, please set the example for this
Younger generation
Don't just teach them right and then you go do wrong
Please lead them all on in the right direction
And if you're in a position, like a politician or a multi-million-dollar man or one of those influential ones
Please let EDUCATION be priority within the budget plan
And let's all fight this life as one Nation with EDUCATION
Every day under committed actions
Toward improving our nation

GANGSTERS

Life's broken mirrors
Negative exposures
Distorted pictures
Blurred all over
The lost righteous features
Reflections obscured
Blocked-out factor
Outright actions of disaster
Careless sorry composure
That self-inflicted terror

Life's evil you render
Breaking lives asunder
Destructive behavior, very costly measure
Wasting life's talented hidden treasure
Insecure thoughts of inferior
Manifested exterior
Putting up and can't break the barriers
Daily it gets harder
More and more by the wee hours
Blaming the system and others
Abused, you become an abuser
Another devil warrior

15 | THOUGHTS OF THE MIND

The drugs no reliever or fast money chaser
Crack, blood money disaster
The life of a gangster, taking lives of others
No different from the black and white oppressor
All killer hustlers, continually taking from the sufferer
Believing you're mega-power
Never protected by the trigger
You're going under, murderers, robbers

Can't run from your inner
From your conscience there's no cover
Your life you torture
Looking over and over your shoulder
Living in that tormented dark corner
Can't take your created sorrow
Nightmares, the flashing fires
Inside fear takes over
Scared to look in the mirror
Only you can change the picture

Trade your evil behavior
Stop the terror
Born-again venture
Glorious real-life makeover
Replace life's broken mirror
Confess and continually say your prayers
Be an exemplary feature
A righteous character

ONLY THE I

Only the I can make it true
The first I
The one and only I
Creation's I
That ruleth I
Supreme I
Father I
Son I
Spiritual I

Davidic I
King I
Fulfillment I
Revelation's I
Zion I
Nations trembling at the sight of the I
Bow ye down to the I
The highest I
The eye's I
Crucified I
Resurrected I
Everlasting I
Israel's I
Jerusalem's I

17 | THOUGHTS OF THE MIND

First singular yes I
Alpha Omega I
One I
That I that created you
That give you rest I
Love I
Jesus Christ the I
Declare rasta for the I
Reigneth I

JAMAICA

Thank God, them did bring them, ya! Jamaica
A beautiful, blessed mountainous area
Surrounded by the clear blue Caribbean waters
Such a natural treasure
An island of rainbow colors
Out of many one people, the nation proudly stands for
The warmth, the hospitality, the amazingly rich ROOTS
Right out of the scripture's culture
A small island of great heroes
People with very high standards, working together for better
The goal-getters don't jester

Great achievers
Blessed believers
Education and morals proper
Universal scholars recognized world all over
As very loving hard, hard workers
Extremely smart, ambitious characters
The Yeh Mon figure
Music-lovers, reggae a them feature
Natives of the land of reggae, wood, and water
Big up agriculture
Good food, natural fruits and juice
Splendid tropical weather
Everything cool-runnings adventure
Strictly no-problem factor

19 | THOUGHTS OF THE MIND

Be a visitor, come, come to Jamaica
Come catch the reggae fever
Hold down a rub-a-dub temperature
Go see the music doctor
Poco jump, skank him order
Stress relievers, nature's doctors
White sands, crystal-clear waters
Go rafting on a river or learn all you can about the amazing
Culture or whatever
Strictly enjoy the irie nature
This African-Caribbean love mixture
Oh, island in the sun, universal pleasure
Jamaica I represent with the highest of honors
As a humble messenger

LOVE

Light of Virtuous Efforts

Oh, can't you see
It's revelation, judgment, prophecy
Thy kingdom come on earth
As it is in heaven
Unification of all God's children
Black, brown, and white
It's the heartodox vibe
'Cause love sees with the heart and not with the eyes
A man's color, it's only a disguise
Feel the love vibes
Real eyes in these times with righteous-
ness, you have got to be baptized
Vibrations from on high
Mankind unite, repentance time
Put hatred, war, all evil aside
Check on inside
Seek and ye shall find
Heartodox mind, spiritual bind
Let the Lord be glorified
And the children be sanctified
Until the color of the skin is way beyond
The color of the eyes
Know ye not the color of the mind
The First Eye is it not color blind
True love that everlasting light
Let righteousness abide

21 | THOUGHTS OF THE MIND

This ain't no choice, surely no dye
Its precious life, and for all He died
Real eyes, sees with the heart and not with the eyes
A man's color is solely a disguise
Heathens mesmerized, love is the eyesight

MARCUS

He wasn't a racist, neither a politician
Only an extremely elevated, educated, culturally ambitious
Proud human
A black man with a mighty vision
A Jamaican sent on a very important mission
The collective security of a nation
The freedom, the unification of all; yes, all Africans
Those at home and those scattered precious remnants
Seeds of the black man

Identification one God, one aim, one destiny
The GAD theory, collective security for all Africans
It's time for repatriation
The solution King David's covenant
Seek ye redemption, salvation
Songs of Solomon
Voices of creation, chants of the black man's land
The dawn of civilization
That true ancient religion
The eternal kingdom
Growl lion, Marcus devotion

Up, ye mighty nation
Ethiopia shall soon stretch forth her hands
Oh, ye seeds of Ham, whence ye came from
Hear the calling lion, calling us home to that promised land
The bread basket of creation
Where it all began
Oh motherland

The direction education, organization, the biblical manifestation
Awaken Africans, understand, fulfill Marcus's vision
Four hundred plus years is much too long
Still sojourners in Babylon
It's time all for the One
Africa's sons and daughters singing the Lord's song
In Jerusalem, the Holy Land
Giving all thanks and praises unto the Almighty One
Bow ye down all nations, united states of Africans

MEN'S

Oppression of these imposed, men made political, religious
Selfish ideologies
It seems only brings misery, poverty, slavery in its madernized category
Minimum wage, cheap labor theory
Brackets controlling the so-called minorities
Daily inhumanities, divisions you see and feel
Self-destructive global crime scene
Those questions, is this for real?
Reality, poverty, man-made disease

Worldwide genocidal catastrophes
Global population poorly in need
Blood money, abortion, murder babies
Murder's huge profiteering industry
Aids, hunger, wars, malaria should not
have taken the lives of so many
And they are still dying numberless daily
Human beings they still sell and steal
Even auction deals
Children for days without a meal
Any and everywhere they sleep
Men made wounds, nations keep
Sweat shops and sex swaps

25 | THOUGHTS OF THE MIND

A disorganized welfare beat
Workers have been feeling the economical heat
Survival of the streets
Life isn't cheap
It's hard still, yet sweet
Give thanks you a breathe

Believe, overcome, and defeat
Learn and yet teach
With love greet
Listen to the world's heartbeat
Beyond barriers reach
Trust in the Lord indeed
Live in grace with one harmony, unity
We are members of one team, human beings
The earth this massive life field
Our greenhouse, keep it clean
Every living thing was meant to be
The power beyond men's theories

What you sow, you'll reap
Set the people free
Collective security the key
Let's all have the same availability
Love, peace, true justice, and equality
Stop being greedy
Share up the wealth, the money
Let's restore the global family
A true loving respectful society
Take heed

The resources to all the people, you must release
In the paths of righteousness we must achieve
Only then will nations truly succeed
You take the lead
Every individual seed
Maintain the fertile greenhouse life field
Like it was meant to be
Keep it real

MOTHERS

Love and deepest respect, along with the greatest of honors to all mothers
Our dearest most valuable world treasure
Always so pure, thy love truly expresses more
Making sure the family is well secure, too often yourself you
Ignore

Your family you always adore
Our ever-caring armor
Earth's angels every hour
That ever-loving protector
Darling of a cure
Ever-prevailing character
With smiles the producer
Your devoted composure

The always-there figure
That knows-best character
Our joyful daily provider
The warmth, ever loving and tender
Very sweet nature
Bearing so much pressure

Your work ceases never
Round-the-clock hours
On call ever
Yet no pay checks to cover
You always fully deliver
Sweethearts, you're the greatest givers
Your love continually showers
The world's number one caretakers, mothers
You're one of life's daily most significant features
Our true gifts from the Almighty Father
We love and cherish mothers for sure ever
Thank you for your love this blessed every day with God's blessings
Love now and forever
MOTHERS

THOUGHTS OF THE MIND

NOT BY THE COLOR

Oh Lord, our Lord
Thou judgeth not by the color
So bring poor people power
Within Your hour
Let Thy blessings shower
Fulfill all our needs
Please hear our humbly plea

We've always fought for our rights
All our lives
While working hard day and night
Trying to live that dream life
Yet a life sentence of poverty is all it seems
It's also criminally real
Who's making and made the biggest steal

We've got to have faith and pray on
And live upright to resist the pressure
By all godly measures
Dear Lord, our Lord
Give us strength by the score
Thy mercies do endure
Tear down these oppressive doors
Let righteousness in for sure
Equality and justice, it's all pure
In Thee, Lord, we do adore

Our cries save the poor
Oh, Lord, only Thou hath secure
Thy children turn to Thee more and more
Our only cure

Oh, Lord, oh, Lord
Thou hath the only answer
Coming with glory and power
And an army of angelic soldiers
Lightning and thunder
Thy wrath shower
Look not over Your shoulder
Earth rent asunder
All immoral acts shattered
Kingdoms devoured
Evil conquered
Feeding the rivers of flaming fire
Thou hath the Deliverer
The righteous within Thy shelter
Abiding forever
Give us clean hearts we continually desire

ONE LOVE FOREVER

With uttermost respect, true love
These feelings so warm and tender
Feelings we now feel today
We've made the vow to keep
Enlarge this true feel for one another
Our union now sealed
Two hearts joined
One heart, one lover forever
One love together
Heart of same desire

This precious holy day we'll cherish, actively remember
As we are now love-abiding life partners
Whatever we face, it's together forever
Shoulder to shoulder
With devotion, love, honor, and all godly features
That great passion for each other
Through good and bad weather
Joy and sorrow
Major or minor
Sweetheart, our true sincere love will always conquer
This wonderful love, our today, our tomorrow
Our dear future
One heart, one lover, together forever

OPRAH

Outstanding **P**erson **R**eaching **A**ll **H**umanity

She's this sensational black toast
And out of poverty, she ambitiously rose
To become a very influential rich host
The Lord enlarges her post
So she brings of the best
Lovingly giving off the most

Unloading from her dear heart
A sister significantly playing her part
Live on the world scene
Fulfilling the dream
Tremendous international scene
Star of the show
An extremely special daily rainbow
As lights of her wisdom glows
Her great knowledge continually flows
The generosity blessedly grows
Reaching way beyond the top of the slope
Throwing the life rope
A black sister bringing hope

33 | THOUGHTS OF THE MIND

The tender love
That driving force of energy
Reaching the world community
A role model giving security
One-of-a-kind personality
You've vastly reached many families
A guide to women, all over creation
You've brought people to fully understand
Your show they successfully lean on
Taking on the world as a black woman
One of high function

On a sincere humanity mission
Remembering where you came from
Only you know that position
It's the Lord, who takes you along, well-conditioned
Beloved sister, stay strong
The world needs your motivation
Keep touching the hearts of nations
Those blessed helping hands
Oprah, thanks
Surely only righteousness will stand
Unto whom much is given
Much is expected of and from

PEACE

The word must fulfill its meaning
And eventually these five letters
Will remain eternally, PEACE
Someday it will be

Poverty **E**liminated **A**chieving **C**omplete **E**quality
Pleaded **E**agerly **A**cross **C**omplete **E**arth
Please **E**nd **A**ll **C**risis **E**arthly
Precisely **E**mbrace **A**ll **C**onfusion **E**rase
Principles **E**nforce **A**im **C**omplete **E**quality
Populations **E**ngage **A**ll **C**ountries **E**ncourage
Positive **E**verlasting **A**im **C**omplete **E**quality
Positively **E**ndure **A**lways **C**onquer **E**ventually
Publicly **E**choing **A**round **C**omplete **E**arth
Prophecy **E**stablished **a** **C**lean **E**arth
Power **E**verywhere **A**ccepting **C**hrist **E**ternally
Prayers **E**ternally **A**lmighty **C**ontrol **E**arth

PEACE

Peace among man and man
Peace to all ye nations
Poverty **E**liminated **A**chieving **C**omplete **E**quality
Peace, world peace

To all those warring factions
Political and religious clans
Stop the extermination plans
Huge profiteering actions, richie, richest distinction
The manufacturing, sales, and distribution of weapons for division and mass destruction
For the battle will be won
He's gonna bring us complete freedom

We are not firing guns in this ya Armageddon
And no, no physical confrontation
It's a spiritual revolution
Fire baptismal
Back off now, Satan
We're under guidance of the Almighty One
And love is the instruction
The Holy Bible the only, only solution in all this confusion
Know the mission
Seek ye salvation

And peace throughout creation
Peace to man and man
People **E**verywhere **A**chieving **C**omplete **E**quality
Peace, world peace

War only brings about destruction
No, no resolutions
Evil intentions
Nuclear desolations
They're heading in that direction
Spending multibillions on weapons
While the world's children are dying for nutrition
Judgment within creation
You've got priority dead wrong

Peace to all ye nations
Peace among man and man
Priority **E**verywhere **A**cross **C**ivilized **E**arth
Peace, world peace

Turn the attention to farming the land
Come on clothe, educate, feed, nour-
ish, and shelter this ya generation
The Gospel of Christ must be preached to all these nations
Remember the resurrection
That everlasting kingdom
Glorify ye in King David's son
Soon revelation
Go spread His Word and fulfill His works among the populations
Righteousness exalteth a nation

And peace to all ye nations
Peace among man and man
People **E**verywhere **A**ccepting **C**hrist **E**ternally
Peace, world peace

SAVE THE CHILDREN

Secure **A**ll **V**irtuously **E**veryon**e** **T**hose **H**umble **E**lite **C**hief **H**umans **i**n **L**ife **D**earest **R**esident**s** **E**nlightening **N**ation**s**

Save the children
This earth's most endangered species
Victims of various brutal abuses
Daily you see the troubled lives
The neglected, sad innocent faces
Secondly thousands of their lives painfully being erase
From poverty, genocide, suicide, abortion,
wars, drugs, starvation, and diseases
Not given a chance to live

Save the children
The nucleus of society
Rejected by their own global preservation authorities
Treated as if they're our enemies
Fill them with true love and generosity
Balance them spiritually
Uplift them morally

To truly uphold show them your responsibility
Give them all the same opportunities
None of them should be in need globally
Fulfill daily their survival, the basic necessities
Put an outright end to wars and poverty
Bring about real justice and equality

Save the children
This world's true royalty
You have all the capacities
Come with loyalty
Release the money
Honesty for the prime of humanity
The children of all countries must be priority
They're our future, nation's destiny
Let's preserve our collective security
Build a world with love and everlasting harmony
Let's raise the living qualities
End the global inhumane atrocities

Save the children
Everyone, especially if you're wealthy
Please show great generosity
It's a global responsibility
Give the children the best of hospitality
Let's create a happy world community
Where the children live free in total safety
All in unity
Well-learned and healthy
Making a difference significantly
Bringing the generations prosperity
Let's enrich society accordingly
End the neglect, please stop the poverty
Save the children, world society
This is a state of emergency
 Serious urgency

RAP

Rich **A**rtistic **P**rogram

Uprising acts
Ghetto's artistic musical plot
From reggae to pop
Great lyrics the original inspirational drop
Cries from the hearts of the have-not
Resisting the poverty trap
Cleanly clearing the block
Positively reaching for the top
No negative prop

RAP
Righteousness **a**lways **p**revaileth
So righteously live and chat
Like the great voices from way back
King David's, King Solomon's beloved chants
Of wisdom tracks
Wisdom never stops
Let's liken the children unto that
The spiritual, moral, uplifting facts
Creating the positive smash
Closing up the poverty gap

RAP
Reaching **A**cross **P**opulations
Saving, enlightening the children
The cream of the crop
Whether brown, white, or black
Unity is a solid rock
Different colors in the same pack
Some placed higher
Majority on the lower rack
Let's level off the pack
Don't keep them back

RAP
Real **A**cademic **P**urpose
Picking up the huge slack
Let's honestly give back
Educating is the rap
Free up the mind strap
Open up the vast thinking slot
A bright light shining
Within all that black
A life-changing voice
On the verbal attack
Today, tomorrow, forever an echoing yap

RAP

Reaching **A**nother **P**erson
Unity our only true collective security act
Education, wisdom, knowledge, understanding
Fill the gap
Let's take nations forward
Equality, love, and Justice on top
Give it all we've got
Make the world one peaceful lot

RAP

Really **A**bout **P**eace

SPINNING AROUND

This earth is spinning around
Mankind now upside down
Heathens continually fight the crown
It's the prophetic age of the evil, old political
Religious clowns
Still wearing the anti-Christ frown
Judgment until whose right to sit the throne
Lord, the children dream of home

The earth is spinning around
Totally being kept down
Confusion, recession in every town
Of the people, black, white, and brown
Societies loosing precious ground
Children gunning nations down
Wars, bloodshed all around
Drugs, immoralities, negativities abound
Negative messages, the air it drowns

The Lord's earth it's spinning around
This world going down
Declare ye fulfill Christ positive sound
Plant ye, invest your seeds within that fertile ground
Let wickedness be bound
Beware of the terror, bloodhounds
Let them be confound
The Lord will bring *all* evil forces down

THOUGHTS OF THE MIND

Earth is spinning around
Significantly melting down
Enormous fires from cities to towns, all around
Now them a clone
Let the lost be truly found
In all this spinning around, upside down
The cries of peace are truly loud
The neglected continually shout
It echoes all about

STAY IN SCHOOL

Spend **T**ime **A**chieving **Y**our **I**ndependently **N**eeded **S**eriously **C**ommitted **H**umble **O**pen **O**pportunities **L**earning

Young men, young women, boys and girls, teenagers
Please play your individual active, ambitious roles
Follow the number one goal
A good education behold
Strengthen your lives, your souls
Education, the major tool
Learning makes life a lot more cool
A good education rules
The priority dude, staying in school

Prevail, graduate
Positively learning opens up a lot of life's gates
Stay in school, the only way
Education is your order every day
Stay **i**n school
Studying **t**oward **a**chieving **y**our
Importantly **n**eeded
Successful **c**ommitted **h**ours **of** **o**pportunities **l**earning
A brighter future it brings

Makes life a lot easier in your daily living
It's that major investment
The most precious time of your life you'll spend
Dedicated daily learning will bring you success
Learn at your best
Learning, earning never rest
Wisdom, knowledge, and understanding *prolongeth*
In life education is that depth
A good education achieveth
Please make it your priority
Honestly get

Education totally embrace
Your talented lives *elevate*
Life's standards continually raise
Learning is an *everlasting* state
Stay in school, immensely it *pays*
Devotion, learning sets the stage
Do it every day
Working hard the only way

STOP THE VIOLENCE

Securely **T**erminate **O**ust **P**unctuate **T**ragic **H**orrible
Events **V**icious **I**ncidents **O**utrageous **L**awlessness
Endangering **N**ations **C**ompletely **E**nd

Our loved ones are our dear treasures
Stop taking their lives with your evil measures
Actions of possessed *monsters*
Child abusers, dope dealers, users, gangsters, murderers, rapers, drunk drivers, black, brown, and white haters
End the covetous crime terrors
The vicious violent horrors

The children need *acts* of joy, not sorrow
They need a better today and tomorrow
A real safe future
Stop the merciless cold disasters
Daily victims from babies to elders
Some dead, others brutally injured
Tearing families asunder
These every day on-going slaughters
Leaving loved ones painfully to suffer
Tremendous loss of mothers, fathers, brothers, and sisters
Taking away *dear* neighbors
Communities scarred forever

Families who never recover
Leaving your own families in torment, some cases extreme danger
It seems violence forever
Revenge here and after
The whole system under pressure
All because of your sad criminal, violent behavior
Violence, crimes very horrible matter

Homies, brothers, and sisters
Whatever your color
The real true factor
Acts of violence will not make you prosper
Taking, ruining, robbing priceless lives will not make you richer
You'll soon be going under
Pay back is what you have sowed; you'll reap over and *over*
Blood money, dope, vanities, and worldly pleasure
Behind your senseless deadly trigger
Your days significantly *numbered*
From your evil self, you can't take cover
Stop being a self-condemned figure

Look deep inside yourself
I know what your conscience says
Repent, all these acts of violence don't make no sense
For surely you'll be recompensed
Reaction tense
Stop the violence, or in the fire you'll be forever spent
Your life totally rent

TALKING DRUMS

True **A**ncient **L**anguage **K**indling **I**nspiration **N**otifying
Gong **D**istinct **R**hythm **U**niversal **M**agnificent **S**ound

Heard from as far as
And way beyond
Echoing throughout creation
Distinct, the talking drums

Backed by humans
Birds, bees, and animals
Flowers, rivers, trees, and seas
All in one continuous combination
Massive percussion
Harmonizing across lands
All earth's musicians
Together every sound in creation

Earth, the universal band stand
It's nature the band
Freedom being sung
PEACE—**p**owerful **e**verlasting **A**lmighty's **c**ommand **e**choing
Heard throughout all nations
Still clear the talking drums being rung

THOUGHTS OF THE MIND

As the sweet melody rises above the trees
Heard across the seas
Echoes carried by the breeze
Cries of world unity
The beat put an end to poverty
Mankind must be free
Save humanity
Faithfully develop society
The sounds rejoicing to the voice of the Almighty
Chorus continually, peace, love, and glory

VIVA, MANDELA, VIVA

Even in death
Sir, you're one of this world's most highly respected, true role figure
A recognized great black leader
Dearly admired universal ambassador
Enormously popular in every corner
One of heavenly character
Always holding your angelic composure
You'll be loved forever
Continually remembered as our global hero

Chief commander
Role scholar
Humble giant of an achiever
You've amazingly broken numberless barriers
While enduring the most brutal of pressure
Making your life that ever-motivating picture
Touching countless lives forever

And viva, Mandela, viva
Live on forever
You've achieved the highest of honors
The number one freedom fighter
Against the racist regime apartheid in South Africa

51 | THOUGHTS OF THE MIND

They cast you in prison because they
thought that you would surely die
Almighty God stood by your side
He prolonged your life
So that you could stand up and topple apartheid

You've caused Pieter Botha to retire
De Klerk came under pressure
Apartheid caught a fire
Runaway slave driver
Majority get their hearts desire
Freedom South Africa

And then you rule, Mandela
With JAH's strength and the people's power
You came much stronger
You're big as a lawyer
The first black prime minister of South Africa
May you always prosper
Dwell in the gates of the Lord forever
Humble, most blessed warrior
Viva, Mandela, viva
Live on forever

WORDS

Works **o**f **R**ighteousness **D**ivine **S**poken

Listen carefully to the message
Your positive reaction, meet
Fulfillment of its reach
Works of the words sent
The heart's desire of its precious need
Emotions of your feelings
That sweet, spiritual, sensational, heart motivating beats

The words' actions, true vibrations you release
Sowing good seeds
Harmony, one sealed deal
Wisdom, knowledge, understanding life's precious shield
Joyful *tremors* of the spiritual feel
Reality of the spirituality

Words teach
Beyond barriers they reach
Another life-changing deed
The word succeeds
It achieves
For everything it heals
Listen carefully, act, oh thee
As the word reveals
It sincerely appeals, come real
Plant prosperity
Truth, the Word, the Almighty

YOUNG GIRLS

Young girls
Precious, priceless black, brown, and white pearls
Live *virtuous* lives
Walk in the light of Jesus Christ
Let Him be your guide

Stay on the safe *side*
Life is not a joy ride
Make the right choice
Be forever respectful and nice
Don't take chances with your lives
Hold your heads real high
With faith and good works, reach unto the sky
Stay clean, humble, and poised
Never be wild

Don't adapt to chasing men, money, and this world's deadly sexual pleasure lifestyle
Your treasured bodies don't spoil
Stay fine, *don't* cross the line
To remain a virgin is the best thing in these times
Young ladies with positive minds
Not the ones giving up their behinds
Next a child having a child

Please wait your matured time
Abstinence isn't a crime
But with STD, you can certainly die
So to yourselves be forever real and kind
Wisdom, knowledge, and understanding truly find
Don't learn the hard way
Precious time lost, when you stray
Young ladies, be safe
Choose the right way
Humbly learn and pray

POEM

Positive **O**bjective **E**nlightening **M**ission

Voice of the mind
Chants of wisdom
Heavenly transmission
Spiritual dictation
Depths of communication
Rhythms eternal

Feelings celestial
Sweet inspiration
Chills of friction
Heart touching vibrations
Irie heights connection
Declaring one and one
Talk, **s**pirit man

Word sound, positive actions
Inward composition
Understand outward mission
The uplifting direction
Heartical expressions
Positive **o**bjective **e**nlightening **m**ission

Meditations alive
Vibes, thoughts that drive high
Pleasant sighs
Sweet heart cries
Reasoning of the unseen voice, way inside
Times telepathic wise
Now, portraits of extreme meditations scribed

Part 2

Sentences Phrases of
Knowledge
Enlightening Nations
Works of Real
Depths Sounded

REAL SIMPLE

Let's make life real simple
By being willing and fully able
To live on His principle
As instructed by the Holy Bible
Be humble

Take the children out of trouble
Show them their bodies are the temple
So help them to overcome the devil
Pick them up when they stumble
Receive Your blessings multiple
Jesus Christ most honorable
Everlastingly favorable

WHAT KIND OF A WORLD

What kind of a world are you living in?
What kind of a world are you living in?
Who makes these laws, yet who keeps them?
The kids not taught to pray
Not taught to pray in these schools
They don't know the Father's rules
Instead they represent different marks of the beast
Keeping all kinds of satanic feast
My God, this is not the least
Tattoos now from head to feet

Men turn to women
And women become men
Church and state even uphold them
Apartheid murder
Abortion legal
Now plans of cloning humans

A world of nuclear weapons
Computerized nations
Robots to replace humans
Multibillion-dollar space missions
While cut back on funding *education*
Humans are dying of starvation
With no place to lay their heads
Cold ground is their daily bed

THOUGHTS OF THE MIND

Is this the plan
To destroy the poor man?
You are heading in the wrong direction
You are heading for your own destruction
What kind of a world are you living in?
What kind a world are we living in?

LIFEGUARD

I am a lifeguard
I am a lifeguard
I am floating in this concrete ocean
Fighting so hard to save my own soul
I am surrounded by vanities of vanities
And vexation of spirits

Dear Lord, guide and protect I
And carry I through these perilous times, my Lord

I am a lifeguard
I am moving through this ya bi ba ba ba bow evil yard
I am surrounded by poverty, segregation
Different acts against humans
Destroying each and everyone
AIDS is on the rampage
And the drugs and crimes have taken all over the place
Such a disturbing disgrace
But I am a lifeguard
Floating through this ya bi ba ba ba bow yard

ONE LOVE DROP

For this you just can't shop
It's a magnetic act
Coming from the extreme top
So no flop
It's a rap
The one love drop

You feel it when it pops
Surely you
Will get attached
A heartical slap
Another heavenly plot
Gathering of the precious crop
The one love drop
I am hooked to that

LOVE CHASE

The true love chase
It's that amazing grace
High spiritual redeeming state
Always replacing hate
True works and solid faith

MAY THE POWERS OF RIGHTEOUSNESS

May the Powers of Righteousness
That brought down South Africa's apartheid
Bring down all oppressive forces within these times
Totally wipe away all bad vibes
Free our minds
Set earth right

May the Powers of Righteousness
Put an end to poverty
The number one crime
Perpetual fire be its fine
Let peace and love abide
Mankind rejoice

May the Powers of Righteousness
Our everlasting guide
The real true light arise
Save the children, the poor innocent lives
Put an end to all the war and strife
Soon worldwide
People we have to unite

HOLY BIBLE

Highest **o**f Literature **Y**eshua's **B**ook in **B**ringing Life Eternity

It's from ancient times given to mankind as an everlasting light
The guidance to an up-full life
This glorious message must be planted heart-wise
Always by your side
The compass of the past, present, and future life
Live the word, the might
Power of our Lord and Savior, Jesus Christ

Read and understand the words
Live a true life
Repent and save your life
Live as a Christ child
Take it to the highest heights
Open up the eyes heart-wise
Love the HOLY BIBLE
The true survival guide
Make your life right
Keep it completely bright
Hold on to the inspiration prescribed for all mankind
Wisdom, knowledge, understanding arise
Let the glory of the Word fill the mind
Heavenly lectures kind

WHAT THIS EARTH NEEDS NOW

Hey, whatever
There's nothing new under the sun, within this huge speculation
And what's going on
A modern world filled with immoral actions
Everything seems to be going wrong, from cloning to abortion
Different forms of destruction
Works of Satan
Dominating within and over man
Mankind can only prevail under one condition

Regardless of your nation
Even your religion
Whatever your race or distinction
Black, brown, white, rich or poor man
We'll soon have to face the same situation
And there's no hiding from the confession
Bow! Oh ye Valley of Decision

Mankind, it's time to truly live and fully understand
There is only one mediator between God and man
The savior of creation
Earth's only protection from even the deadliest of weapons

And what this entire earth needs now
Is Yeshua, Jesus Christ
Yeshua, Jesus Christ is not just only for some
But Lord of everyone
He gave His life a living ransom not just for some
But hope for everyone
Revelation, conclusion, come now, Lord Jesus Christ

THE SIGNIFICANT BIRTH

Way beforehand, it was highly prophesied
Yet no one knew the appointed time
It was ordained from on high
The only conception like this you will ever find
Only one truly kind
The Blessed Virgin Mary pregnant not by man
But spiritual-wise

Joseph never lost his mind, causing no war and strife
He did what was right
Took care of his wife
Stood by her side
In the Lord he did abide

Then that joyous night
The heavens shone so amazingly bright
Shepherds got the message by the angel's voice
As wise men carrying gifts travelled for miles
Guided by the star to behold the Most Blessed Child

The Savior of the world born at a barn outside
Angels sung and the animals rejoiced
To behold the lamb-lion in their sight
The everlasting light
Power and might
The Holy Child, ever meek and mild

They all glorified
Peace tonight
Joy to the world
Let thee Creator arise
On earth in the flesh, He has arrived.
Son of God
Breath of Life

FATHERS

Fathers, you are our ever special human beings by the Creator
Not just seed-throwers
But devoted, pure, caring farmers
Excellent supporters
Those always there for the children and mothers
Lifetime active lead players
You are our mentors
Blessed molders of the past, present, and glorious future
Earth's strongest role authoritative figures
Natural-born real leaders
Head providers
Striving devotedly to make life much better

Excellency of His power
Our highly overlooked daily heroes
Great workers, society's builders
Thanks immensely for being those always mightily strong characters
With those huge uplifting backbone and shoulders
Our dear loving shelters
Throughout all life's weather

In His image continually represent the Almighty Father
His blessings, highest of love and dearest of honors
We look unto you, our guiding stars forever
Continually laying those solid, secure structures
Our amazing motivators
Those enduring, brave, ambitious, proud lifetime changers
You are our highly respected, deeply loved fathers

MOTHERS

Most **O**utstanding **T**rue **H**eroes **E**arth's **R**eplenishing **S**uperstars

The greatest of all lovers
Their love ceases never
Earth's best caregivers
Always there to answer
On-call twenty-four hours
Dearest of all responders
Their schedules seems never over
Life's ever adoring, tender figures
The world's best providers

Universe's most angelic characters
Making the world far much happier
With those kindly supporting, strong, sweet composures
They lovingly endure all the everyday pressures
Truly amazing burden bearers
Keeping it all together

Life's number one supporters
Extremely blessed survivors
Too often double role players, mother and father
Our precious leaders of the past, present, and future
Darling dear mothers
Our everyday global teachers
Life's true heroes
Mothers

Don't Drink And Drive. Death.

Definitely **O**h **N**o **T**hing **D**riving **R**isk
Intoxication **N**otorious **K**iller
Avoid **N**ever **D**rive
Deadliest **R**uins **I**ntoxicated **V**ehicular **E**ngagements
Dreadful **E**nd **A**lcohol **T**ragedies **H**orrific

Never defy
Decline every time
Why be the next one to kill, be arrested, or die?
In this state at no time are you fine
You can't fool the mind
Just can't hide
It's a risk, much too high
Plus a serious crime
With consequences never kind

Another death dive
Don't deprive
It's a process of suicide
Or another life flight
Clinging for life
Because of your careless lifestyle
Children seriously painfully denied
Family's tragic loss and tormented cries
Foolish terrible costly price

Make the right choice
There are other means to depart
Most importantly to safely arrive
Decide on catching a ride
Be always on that safe side
Stay happy and correctly alive
Stop taking innocent lives
Happy hour is protecting and enjoying lasting life
Please don't drink and drive

PRAISE MAN

It's a saving-souls mission
You feel the miraculous devotion
A true reaching hand
Changing lives situation
Praise Man
Houston's daily vital heart-touching inspiration
On Christian station 92.1
Spiritual communication
Uplifting vibrations
Across the nation
Check in, turn it up, praises
Unto the Almighty One
Coming from Robert Washington "Praise Man"
Exalting the Great I Am man

GOD'S CHILD

Yes, you're God's child
An earthly angel sent by the divine
Inside and outside, you're amazingly fine
Solid body and mind

That admirable smile
Those healing hands from the divine
Individuals like you are too hard to find
One of those kind

Those wishes of mine
Baby, it's your time
Leave trouble behind
Don't ignore the warning signs
Stop playing blind
Wanting the best is not a crime
Live in the positive vibe

Oh, let the Lord strengthen your mind
Remember God is the prime
And you're His loving child
Stay on the safe side
His hands are always open wide
His Words the everlasting light
He's the choice

BULLY

Busted **U**p **L**ife **L**ost **Y**ours

Another waste-of-life-and-time story
And it's so sorry
Because your deeds aren't funny
Just a severe menace to society
End your heart-breaking acts of brutality
Those you inflict upon the less fortunate and those of diversity
Within our schools and communities
You've brought about so many tragedies, mentally and physically
You're painfully, abusively destroying and disrupting lives daily
Showing no sympathy
Seeking negative attention continually
Believing you're above everybody
Defying all authority
You're just plain misery
End your stupidity now, bully
Before you end up in the cemetery much too early

You think it's silly, or is it your evil jealousy?
It's your sickening immaturity, careless arrogancy and ignorancy
You even abuse your own body
Leaving lifelong scars, destructive memories
Hard roads to recovery
Deeply affecting families
But eventually, bully, you'll be paid accordingly
Devoted acts of love is the only remedy

THOUGHTS OF THE MIND

Stop preying on our families
Turn your life around significantly
Repent and serve the Almighty
Use your energy positively
Have much respect for yourself and humanity
If you want to fight, go join the army
Ambitiously guide your destiny
Love thy neighbor as thyself unconditionally
Live to make a better society
To make peace, it's our daily responsibility
Builders for a better global community
Make a loving impact upon history
Stop being a bully
Truly honor your fellowman and your country
Please act intelligently, stop being a bully immediately

SISTERS

To the beloved sisters universally
Mothers and ye young girls to be
In the Almighty ye must glory
Know your priority
Don't be hasty to give up your virginity
Wait until you marry

It's all about maturity
Adopt rich qualities
Place yourself in the angel category
You're worth far more than diamonds and rubies
Priceless is a virtuous lady
She's devoted to her family
A one-man woman only
Of a God-fearing personality
In the Lord she's always happy
And she knows whose baby
Doesn't need a DNA test for Tom, Dick, or Harry
Only one man sees her body
She's filled with purity
Serving the Lord continually

SUPERMAN

Supreme **U**niversal **P**ower **E**xalting
Righteousness **M**aster **A**bove **N**ations

The truth, not fiction
Now that I am grown
I have come to love, know, and understand who is SUPERMAN
The universal-soul man
The real great hero
The role model of nations
Master, ruler of all creation
That rides upon the wings of the wind without any motion
Having the whole world in His hands
Whose coming was so significant, angels sang

SUPERMAN, born of the Spirit
The Only Begotten Son
The Almighty One
Only sinless man
Power of redemption
That everlasting kingdom
He came on the greatest mission
To save that promised generation
The Great Physician
Never weak, forever strong

Only always S-man
Savior of all creation
The Man, the Great I Am
Mankind salvation
Showed us the right direction
Filled with love and affection
Taught us to seek heavenly possessions
He overcame persecution and the death situation
Wiped away our sins and transgressions
The Crucifixion and His glorious resurrection
Thy kingdom come
Oh, SUPERMAN's revelation
Sign of the time's condition
To rid earth of corruption
Most of all, to conquer Satan
SUPERMAN, the meek lamb
The humble, conquering lion
His mercy, His grace, His name, His work goes on and on and on
He's the joy of all creation
Let's follow His actions
Rescue us soon please, SUPERMAN

OBAMA

Our **B**lackness America **M**ust **A**ccept—
One **B**lood America's **M**an African
Our **B**rother's **A**cceptance **M**ajor **A**chievement

A statement to world society
Shadows of destiny
One of the significant moments of the century
President Obama's major victory
The people's responsibility
This nation's majority accountability
Change the category, but it's still politics
Another great chapter of black history
Well-observed by the global community
A nation's proud, significant story
Touching lives, change of many
Proving there's always a possibility

Sweet, sad memories of how things used to be
A race's negative journey
Overcoming diversity
Exploding out of poverty
Up, black child of slavery
Black and white, ebony
A brother filled with positive energy
Who never lost his identity
Beloved publicly
To offer he's got plenty
Such a humble personality
Setting examples for other countries

Now this black man's well-watched opportunity
Leader of the free world's largest territory
An African holding up America's presidency
Something we thought we would never see
The White House black residency
Black people, the First Family
Strong figures of authority, with very successful rich qualities
Alarming capabilities
Amazing abilities, educated at Harvard University
Deeply respected politically
Having a goal of global unity
World peace priority

As we face recovery
Everyone involve strategy, together the theory
Brother remember the political dirty
I know you're feeling the racist sabotage policy
Put your trust only in the Almighty
His policy priority
Yes, Christianity; no, partiality
Let the spirit rule eternally
Lead this nation triumphantly
Uphold morally
One **B**lood **A**lmighty **M**ade **A**ll
Organized **B**lessed **A**rticulate **M**agnificent **A**chiever
Our **B**rother's **A**chievement **M**iraculous **A**ccomplishment

CHRIST

They keep on wanting us to deny
But with Him we truly identify
He's the Savior of our lives
And no powers, no might
Cannot put out the eternal light
So stop the fight
Our everlasting right is to continually praise and exalt
Our Lord and Savior, Jesus Christ

At all times strive always to be by His side
He's our only true guide
Master of everlasting life

YARD PEOPLE

Dearly beloved brothers and sisters of that beautiful area
Famously known as Jamaica
Let's make our island that ever blessed
Cool-runnings international feature
By first going forward into our ROOTS
Right out of the scriptures culture
Living, showing the world we are true believers
Children of that kingdom established forever
Part of that glorious treasure
Upholding the works of Marcus Garvey, Bob Marley, and
The teachings of the emperor
Fulfilling the roles of our great teachers
Inspiring messengers
Carrying high the banner of the Almighty Father
His way of life we must completely follow

One blood come together
Regardless of the poverty pressure
Unity is power
Let us always love one another
End all the political slaughters
Regardless who is ruler
Respect always for each other
Together we suffer
Stop the vicious robberies, halt the cold-blooded murders
We're tearing our own bond asunder with all the negative behavior

Weapons of war, drugs were made to make poor people even weaker
Lessen our numbers
Using our own family members as deadly players of divide and conquer
Shoulder to shoulder let's ease the pressure
Let's end the man-made disasters
Create for our children that bright future
Be that highly ROOTS character
Rich in heavenly stature
Humble, working hard to make his homeland better
True onward Christ-like soldier
Upholding humanity's true culture
One love, one heart, always the order
Let yard fully prosper

Be a peace maker
Real farmer
Spiritual and physical planters
Good seeds plant all over
Big up agriculture in the land of wood and water
Feed the worldwide consumers
Be a positive-vibe carrier
A royal ambassador
Hold down your corner
Yard man, positive figure
Only righteousness endures forever
Fight life with godly measures
Solid partaker
Rise up, sweet, blessed Jamaican producers
Let love shower

TIGER WOODS

Totally **I**nto **G**olf **E**xceptional **R**oots
Winner **of** **O**utstanding **D**istinction **S**pecial

Hard work, hard labor, and a determined youngster
Practicing for hours
Hitting the white ball over, yonder, and under
Tearing down barriers
Creating a disaster
Number one golfer
Tiger, the amazer

Born of African-Asian culture
His dad the instructor
Mom the inspirer
Both parents, great motivators
A three-year-old putter
Tremendous learner getting his game together
Making of a winner, positively directing his future

Master teenager, most knowledgeable
The game's star, number one figure
Dominating the amateurs, so up the ladder, taking on the majors
With supreme power, trendsetter
What an astonishing crossover, as you come on stronger and better
The best, happy days, hard labor

Times very well spent
That now a rare historic sport event, seen world all over
Multimillion viewers getting it direct in real color
A dynamic sport's treasure, one to forever remember
Twenty-one-year-old Tiger Woods taking on the Masters
Golf's century record-breaker
Fulfilling heart's desire, revealing game composure
Move over to the shoulder, the game is getting the needed flavor
And he's the world feature

Tiger Woods, the cool dude, trampled the hood
Alone he stood, receiving the green jacket
Crashing yet another bracket
Brother, you just took it, much to the fit
A major worldwide lift

Seizing the attention of the world, capturing boys and girls
Attracting vast admirers, you took golf sport over
A true world hero
An open winner, what's up, number one player
World conqueror, golf's total power
The brown and black figure, ever ready to devour
Setting records over and over
You're a leader; in you many sees hope
And gets stronger and stronger
Working hard to become an achiever like Tiger
To watch you play, it's a true great pleasure

USAIN BOLT

Let it be told, as history unfolds
The fastest human being the world has ever behold
Usain Bolt, Jamaica's natural well-bred
Sprinting colt

Out from the blocks he floats
A gliding human speed boat
Full throttle as he goes, about to cut throats
Swiftly flying lightning bolt
Represent yellow, black, and green coat
A Fe We Gold

World, 100m and 200m records broke
Jamaica hold, man, you bold
Keep on running them cold
You're a one-man world show
They love to see you go
Yard man smoothly flow
Run under your cover
Usain Bolt has taken over
A real human, natural motor

To his talent he devotes
A very special mold
Sand and hills training, superior control
With mark, set, and go
Witness a human lightning roll
Accomplishing his goal

ABORTION

Another **B**aby **O**utrageously **R**uthlessly **T**erminated
Inhumane **O**peration **N**umberless

Those stifling tiny cries
As another one dies
Those killings are so very high
Society, Mr. M. D., why?

It don't need no Supreme Court–special session
No amendments of the Constitution
Away with the *Rhode versus Wade* decision
Fire for any religious confirmation
Endorsed by which political clan
Stop the demonstrations
Why the physical confrontations
End all the violent actions
It's already a grave situation
Innocent blood upon the land
Mankind knows it's totally wrong, destruction

Against the laws of creation, from whence ye came from
Stop slaughtering off the little ones
Your profiteering murder plan can't control the population
Abortion viciously wrong
Extreme suffocation
Utterly immoral situation
Another mystery of Babylon

This is no solution
A devil mission, execution of the little ones
What is your profession?
To save lives or to take thousands
Mr. Physician, are you a licensed killer man
Stop all the abortions, your blood money can't keep you for too long
And His judgment is at hand
You'll have to face the Chief Physician
Fire your prescription
The wrath of the Almighty One
Abortion's reaction

SAY NO, NO TO DRUGS

Strictly **A**gainst **Y**ou **N**egative **O**bjects
Never **O**kay **T**otally **O**bstructive
Deadly **R**isk **U**ndergoing **G**rave **S**uffocation
DRUGS RACE
Deadliest **R**uins **U**niversal **G**rave **S**ituation
Running **A**cross **C**omplete **E**arth

It's a major topic every day
An international affair
High crime rates, it seems all our lives are at stake
As weapons ablaze
Drugs sets the stage
Drugs war cover, the daily news page

The running of the drugs race
Here it's running from state to state
Maybe within your gate
No time to debate
Blood money rage
Death the highest stake
Continuous deadly take
Your enemy could be your mate

Little children, young men, young women, don't be no bait
Never join the fast money, deadly chase
Be good, keep the faith
Positively create

Drugs will leave you in your final resting place
It has no respect for age
Too often you end up in jail, sometimes no bail
Another life about to fail
Huge criminal trail
Life please don't waste
Don't live this way
Daily, secondly, crazily people get their high
Minutely they fall, oh so sadly they die
It's so grave

Man-made plague, they crave to the grave
Serious is no play, kids selling dope
Sometimes families only hope, hope in dope
Yet dope has no hope
It's a slow fatal choke
Death's no joke
Too tight a real rope
Not knowing what they sell, what they smoke
It could be their last sale, their last stoke
Back where they started, cold and broke
Continuous sliding off the deadly slope, find hope
Drugs race, death steeple chase
Too fatal a blow
Make your life an enlightening show
Love bestow
Peace of mind glows
Let righteousness flow

CRACK

Creating Ruins another Cold Killer

Hands off that
Don't, don't, don't
I beg you people
Please don't do that
The name tells a lot
Crack
Creating ruins another cold killer

It's a fact
Leaving people sadly on their backs
A very sad mock
Serious laughing stock
Part of an evil vicious death plot
Life a flop
Messing with crack
People don't, don't do crack

It's a deadly, cheap treat
Knocking so many off their feet
Having them living in the streets
Nothing to eat
You become a thief
Anyone you'll cheat
Your life a total defeat
Heart missing beats

Loss of teeth
Heart attack
As another one drop
Withered away from crack

So don't, *please* don't
Touch that killer crack
Why lack?
Out on the cold block
Vital signs flat
Stay away from the death trap
Crack

STRIVE

STRIVE
NFL
TARGET
NOW OK YOU
STAY IN SCHOOL
NBA
EDUCATION
STUDY
READ
LEARN
MATHS
GRADUATE
COLLEGE
FOCUS
WNBA
NHL
EDUCATION

Seek **T**ruth **R**ighteously **I**nspired **V**irtuously **E**nlightened
Never **F**lunk **L**ife
True **A**im **R**eal **G**oal **E**ducation **T**oday
Nature **O**f **W**isdom **O**btain **K**nowledge
Your **O**bjective **U**nderstanding
Spend **T**ime **A**chieving **Y**our
Importantly **N**eeded
Seriously **C**ommitted **H**umble **O**pen **O**pportunities **L**earning

No Better Accomplishment
Every Day Under Committed Actions
Towards Improving Our Nation
Striving Towards Uplifting Developing You
Receiving Every Academic Dimension
Lessons Embrace Academics Real Necessity
Master All This Huge Sum
Great Responsible Accomplishment Daily
Upliftment Achievement Toward Excellency
Collectively Obtaining Lasting Lessons
Establishing Gain Experience
Forward On Creating Ultimate Success
Winners Never Back Away
No Higher Learning
Enlightening Developments Under Christian
Actions Triumphantly Inspiring Our Nation

WNBA

Winners **N**ever **B**ack **A**way

Hip, hip, hoorah
Hey, winners never back away
Learning brings vast gain
Devotion to hard work, less play
Learning is the order each day
From school never stray
Sacrifice is to appreciate
Studying elevates life in extremely special ways
Win this game is to graduate
On to expanding your intake
A great career make
Life you can't fake

It's what you achieve today
The solid foundation you lay
Developed moments of study and pray
Going to school every day
Giving your best in every way
The good habits you shape
Learning now is the prosperity later on you'll joyfully face

Winners never back away
The whole course they stay
Well-equipped for life's play
Positively create

Education you must fully embrace
Win life's steeple chase
Learning is an everlasting state
Read, study away, balancing your pace
Knowing the aim
A winner every day, filled with grace
Keeping the faith

ACKNOWLEDGMENT

Uttermost highest of praises unto Jesus Christ, the only Lord God!

Thanks to my parents, George and Edna Kinghorne, for imparting excellent values and morals upon us.

Deepest of love and respect to Sam and Paulette Kinghorne, my two siblings still here out of six children.

God's blessings upon my son, grandsons, also Sasha, Christopher, Damian, and their families.

Immense love for everyone who has been a part of my life, especially those I've lived with. Thanks! Blessings to Tricia, Tammy, Trevor, Kayli, Laketa, LJ, Vilma, Georgia, Sheila, Tiara, Trinity Shiloh, Sunshine, Noel, and his family.

Felipito, you will not be forgotten; look into God's bright future. Magnet love always. Soon you'll find complete true love, peace, joy, and everlasting light in Christ.

Thank you Sandra Winzer for everything.

Special gratitude for His Imperial Majesty Emperor Haile Selassie I, Dr. Vernon Carrington Gadman, Pastor Dr. Freddie Parham, Ph.D., First Lady Parham, and everyone at Word of Faith Church. Great role players in Jesus Christ.

Thanks unto God for His greatness, using me as His vessel in this work. It's His will.

To Stephanie, Angella, Jeanie, Margret, Madge, Linda, Lesa, Olga, Sharon, my brethren and sisters all over earth, God's guidance and love.

Page Publishing and its great workers, thanks!

ABOUT THE AUTHOR

Reggie Naphtali was born Reginald Kinghorne in Kingston, Jamaica, to George and Edna Kinghorne. He attended St. Aloysius, St. George's College, Excelsior evening classes, and Boy's High, Brooklyn, New York. He left Jamaica in 1983 to reside in America, but he has never strayed or forgotten his deep roots.

CPSIA information can be obtained
at www.ICGtesting.com
Printed in the USA
FFOW02n0243280517
35982FF

9 781683 484813